The Strange Weiner Dog

A Coloring Book

DR. B.B. HIGHTOWER

ARCHWAY PUBLISHING

Archway Publishing books may be ordered through booksellers or by contacting:

Archway Publishing
1663 Liberty Drive
Bloomington, IN 47403
www.archwaypublishing.com
844-669-3957

ISBN: 978-1-6657-3322-9 (sc)
ISBN: 978-1-6657-3323-6 (e)

Print information available on the last page.

Archway Publishing rev. date: 12/14/2022

This Book belongs to

MY WEINER DOG STORY:

MY WEINER DOG STORY:

HA-HA-HA

MY WEINER DOG STORY:

MY WEINER DOG STORY:

MY WEINER DOG STORY:

MY WEINER DOG STORY:

MY WEINER DOG STORY:

MY WEINER DOG STORY:

MY WEINER DOG STORY:

MY WEINER DOG STORY:

MY WEINER DOG STORY:

ANGE
DOG

MY WEINER DOG STORY:

MY WEINER DOG STORY:

MY WEINER DOG STORY:

Thank you for my weiner dog...Amen
Thank you for ice cream... Amen

MY WEINER DOG STORY:

MY WEINER DOG STORY:

MY WEINER DOG STORY:

Weiner dog, where are you!

MY WEINER DOG STORY:

MY WEINER DOG STORY:

WOOF
WOOF

MY WEINER DOG STORY:

MY WEINER DOG STORY:

MY WEINER DOG STORY:

MY WEINER DOG STORY:

MY WEINER DOG STORY:

MY WEINER DOG STORY:

MY WEINER DOG STORY:

MY WEINER DOG STORY:

"Oh, Holy Night..."
?

MY WEINER DOG STORY:

"Oh, Holy Night…"

MY WEINER DOG STORY:

SUGAR
FLOUR

MY WEINER DOG STORY:

SUGAR
FLOUR
TEA

MY WEINER DOG STORY:

MY WEINER DOG STORY:

MY WEINER DOG STORY:

Bark, woof, bark, woof!!! What is the reason for this joyous season?

MY WEINER DOG STORY:

MY WEINER DOG STORY:

Oh, come all ye Faithful.

MY WEINER DOG STORY:

Thank you, for my family, Lord.

Printed in the United States
by Baker & Taylor Publisher Services